TENDER TO
THE QUEEN OF SPAIN

Ken Smith was born in 1938 in Rudston, East Yorkshire, the son of an itinerant farm labourer. He has worked in Britain and in America as a teacher, freelance writer, barman, magazine editor, potato picker and BBC reader, and has held writing fellowships at Leeds University, Kingston Polytechnic, and Clark University and Holy Cross, Worcester, Massachusetts. From 1985 to 1987 he was GLA writer-in-residence at Wormwood Scrubs prison. He lives in East London.

Smith's first book, *The Pity*, was published by Jonathan Cape in 1967, and his second, *Work, distances/poems*, by Swallow Press, Chicago, in 1972. Poems from these two collections and from a dozen other books and pamphlets published between 1964 and 1980 (including *Fox Running*) were brought together in his Bloodaxe Selected Poems, *The Poet Reclining* (1982; reissued 1989), which does not include work from *Burned Books* (1981) or his later Bloodaxe titles.

In 1986 Ken Smith's collection *Terra* was shortlisted for the Whitbread Prize. In 1987 Bloodaxe published his collected prose, *A Book of Chinese Whispers*. His last four poetry collections, *Terra* (1986), *Wormwood* (1987), *The heart, the border* (1990) and *Tender to the Queen of Spain* (1993) have all been Poetry Book Society Recommendations.

In 1989 Harrap published *Inside Time*, Ken Smith's book about imprisonment, about Wormwood Scrubs and the men he met there. This was published in paperback by Mandarin in 1990.

Ken Smith was working in Berlin when the Wall came down, writing a book about East and West Berlin: this turned into *Berlin: Coming in from the Cold*, published by Hamish Hamilton in 1990 and in paperback by Penguin in 1991. He edited the anthology *Klaonica: poems for Bosnia* (Bloodaxe Books, 1993) with Judi Benson.

TENDER TO
THE QUEEN
OF SPAIN

KEN SMITH

BLOODAXE BOOKS

ISBN: 1 85224 261 2

First published 1993 by
Bloodaxe Books Ltd,
P.O. Box 1SN,
Newcastle upon Tyne NE99 1SN.

Bloodaxe Books Ltd acknowledges
the financial assistance of Northern Arts.

Cover printing by J. Thomson Colour Printers Ltd, Glasgow.

Printed in Great Britain by
Bell & Bain Ltd, Glasgow, Scotland.

*Imagination and memory are but
one thing, which for divers considerations
hath diverse names.*

THOMAS HOBBES
Leviathan

Acknowledgements

Acknowledgements are due to the editors of the following publications in which some of these poems first appeared: *Active in Airtime, Acumen, Ambit, Bête Noire, The Blue Nose Anthology, Eletunk* (Hungary), *Foolscap, Great River Review* (USA), *The Guardian, The Independent, Kalligram* (Slovakia), *Klaonica: poems for Bosnia* (Bloodaxe Books, 1993), *The Mencard Series, Oxford Magazine, Poetry Review, Poetry Wales, Poetry with an Edge* (Bloodaxe Books, second edition, 1993), *The Rimbaud Centenary, The Rialto, Sunk Island Review, Stand, Stride* and *Turret Books Broadsides.*

Contents

Tender to the Queen of Spain

In the foreground there is the large row boat upside down on trestles, being scraped and repainted by two men in the working sunlight of the harbour, a spring afternoon, in Weymouth. Seen upside down, so that my head must tip to read it, its name says it's the tender to a larger boat, not visible anywhere amongst the other boats of the small port – lighters, trawlers, coastal barges, fishing trip and pleasure boats, yachts, old coalers painted up with their brown sails slack in the intermittent wind, sail boats tinkling like a mad orchestra of only cymbals. Our boat is not amongst them. She is out chugging on the huge sea, with an unknown cargo for unknown destinations, for who knows how long, and all we know of her is her name: *The Queen of Spain.*

Milly's end

She died. Worse was her undoing,
the tongue's unravelling, the memory's flat battery

coughing in the night *someone has taken my orange juice,*
someone has stolen my shoes. Up,

down, either was difficult, *it's not*
her any more I hear my voice say again

through the narrowing months of her vision
that could see bright clear to a winter day.

There was a war, she worked in the harvest
of wet beets, soldiers came in and out her gate,

in and out of her kitchen, hot white mugs
in their hard cold hands.

Where are they all now? she asks.
How many ever came back?

The other elegy

...i.m. Asa *(foolish enough*
to have been a poet) Benveniste, the tall
skinny tree of you felled in the churchyard
at Heptonstall among the Queen Anne's Lace.

It was a Friday, it was the thirteenth,
sunset, Easter, and you you would have
timed it differently, you would have sat
right down and writ yourself a letter.

This is for all the lives we did not live,
mooching in old harbours with the tides,
driving home across the rainswept moorland,
drunk, remembering Brooklyn, Amsterdam.

At the border will be stones and again
white birches, the one magpie of sorrow,
you in your black cap surprised and amused,
you with two flowers where the road runs out.

The painter Mannfred Otto

He is a painter, time indeterminate. Europe.
Then. Also a husband, father, neighbour.
Burgher of the town he was born in, a citizen.

Self-portraits, mostly. Masks, in various light,
shadow so, various moods, different stages of his life.
Certain moments he was drawn to paint:

his message to the woman he'd marry he'd not met yet,
in his hand a sprig of rosemary. A flat faced boy,
the young soldier, a wanderer, mid-life, old age.

The day he won the old quarrel with Sartorius.
The years of invasion, famine, the great death.
Mother, wife, children, all at once gone.

What he couldn't paint: the black rump of night
where there's no point to the dawn, no purpose
for him in the sun's ever again coming up.

And the outrage of birdsong, the dawn chorus
a panic in the chest, acid on the tongue.
And who let all this sudden white light in here?

Self portrait in shadow. Self portrait in sorrow.
Self portrait with fruit and flowers.
Self portrait with instruments and cats.

Slowly: outside events: astrolabe, compass,
half finished block of stone, the texts
in the vernacular he lived by, a white bird.

Sheaf of gathered wheat. A stuck pig.
Baskets of dark grapes. Like so. On the hills bonfire smoke,
autumn woods, towers of the city. Cloud etched to rain.

Jack remembering

Out walking the hill's side, the wind here
smashes the saplings, no trees,
no tree cover, nowhere to hide now,
the old stones taken for walls and roadwork.

Above these grey towns, streets I don't know,
a corner the road goes where trees gathered
that are gone now. So much sky then,
the stars scattered milk, the silence.

I lived beyond this, in my own house,
with a yard and garden, trees, chickens, a pig,
two goats and the white doves, all my days
I made a rough worsted, the same gun metal grey.

Home from the wars I was handsome and workshy,
a green stone on a ring was mine once,
that came from the Nile. Another took it,
thereafter into the ground with him.

I was a good soldier, bright buttons,
bulled webbing and boots, knife crease
in tunic and trews, I was always on parade,
on the march, on manoeuvre, on a drunk, or asleep.

No, I'm not mad. I have this wound, Doctor,
I call Ivan the Terrible, it bleeds when the wind's
from any direction, winter and summer. It weeps
but I don't know for what grieving.

What else I recall are tiny white roses
growing in the Basques' country of the tongue.
And wayside herbs: feverfew, yarrow,
soldier's wort, all good for something.

Brother Scratchwood

Where I am: in the far black of the cave
of my self, in the dark that was never lit,
which is to say nowhere, among the unwritten,
the *agrapha*, who live in the mountains
and pay no taxes and therefore do not exist.

My life an alphabet of edges,
smoke around a taper, my eyes are not good,
only a vague ache now where I used to be.

I've hung out in the empty spaces between lives,
through slow winter dusks, decade by decade
through seasons of nothing but patience patience,
in the nowhere wherein I imagined *nothing*.

And went mad with the thought of it.
God knows there's not much of me,
light enough to be someone, anyone by,
peering into a name *Brother Scratchwood*, for instance.

Who waits the way iron waits, and the stars,
the way flame sleeps in the wax, the cast
in the dice, mumbling my interminable prayers,
kyrie eleisons to my own wayward heartbeat.

Night after night, all night long,
my arse crossed on the misericorde's edge,
where Moses crossing the Red Sea sniffs
the wind of thin farts come of piety's porridge.

And that's all there is of me, stoney hours
left and right of me my brothers on our knees
calling à cappela in the empire of the dark
crowding to one candle's flame. Amen.

One of Milly's gifts

Sometimes one of Milly's gifts gets drunk,
makes a fool an absolute asshole of himself,
comes home late and stormy and breaks things,
mostly his own things. And next morning

can't remember any of it. He's sorry
but he doesn't know what for. He can't tell
who the enemy is and he doesn't have any friends.
There's a list hereabouts he's not on it.

His subscription's cancelled. In the dawn,
sleepy, bladder heavy, the first of the birds
waking in the blue light of his brain,
he gets up, discovers just all the books

floating in the bathtub, and the kitchen
covered in broken blue and white crockery
and the wife of those years saying *Why?*
Why do you do these dreadful things?

Three in a play

Three cardplayers
in a game of three:
Stick, Twist, Trump.

Three lords of the dance,
Thump, Boot, Headbutt,
rough tongued and tattooed, three liebknechte.

Freelance, hitmen, anyone's.
Anyone: that huddle at the door,
three fiddlers about to play the Fire Hose Reel.

Three men in a tub.
Three drunks in a pub.
Three dark eyed assassins.

The three gold-tongued knights of the court
of King Arthur, three horsemen
who are Dürer's knight, death, the devil.

Umbilicus, the young naval attaché,
Scrotum, the wrinkled old retainer,
Sputum, a Flemish outcast.

Three separate faces
on the night bus, that follow you home,
and know where you live now.

Woman without a name

Passing on the stairs, what to say to her,
lost in the blue hazy spaces
of the beautiful distance of herself? Say:
You're very kind. And very beautiful.

Decades ago, in an ill-lit guttural city,
where I, exiled, cold, smoking my black cheroots,
stalked the winter park, feeding the water birds,
my academic study life at the water margins.

And that's the whole of the affair, her heels
clacking up the stairwell, the elevator
out again, the winter night, the corner
where she turns clockwise out of my life forever.

It's late, and this is where the door turns in.
Her name her name if I could think of it.
The luxury of a name, and through it swifts,
in the high trees the rooks squabble.

Coffee, little cakes. I take her picture out
remembering her as she was not, forget-me-nots
knotted in her fingers, frowning
into the old box brownie, so long ago.

Part of something else

Turalura she sings to herself, breathing
in, out, him staring into the fireback
numbering his grumbles, his what he now
only wished he'd said then but thought
too late, later, the moment gone.

Turalura, turalura. As for her
the bread she bakes is soon stale,
his side of the bed always lumpy,
her sex cold dry inhospitable, then
his inventory of misery begins, *cunt cunt.*

Turalura, lureia. She knows the moment
he's wound himself up and the wire hisses out of him,
taut, barbed, edged, and it's thereabouts
she'll go up, go to sleep in her white sheets
mumbling *Is there any wonder? Turalura.*

Later in the tea-room

I could believe, a moment or two,
there in the cathedral with the candles
and soaring through the tall stones
the music of the choir and the organ.
And all those dear dead battered bishops.

I think Heaven must be like this:
feathery quiet and old flowers,
weightless light and long webby nothings,
stones made of cloud, soft rain and warm snow,
ice cream you'd never get sick of.

Consider John Longland, 1521-47
Bishop of Lincoln, Confessor
to Henry the Eighth. And consider
what griefs what regrets what bottomless bragging
he must lie with, centuries thereafter.

The blue time

Saturday the storm. She left early,
in her pink shoes skipping down the road.
She'd dreamed of candyfloss, roses,
her mother's wild chrysanthemums.

Time for a walk and a stare at nothing.
Time for tea and hot buttered scones, a turn or two
through the wild wind of the garden
savouring lavender, thyme, angelica.

It's the blue time in the season's swift changes,
flagged once by the first cornflower,
twice by the first blue star of the borage,
a message to foxgloves and the tall white daisies:

solstice and midsummer, harvest then winter,
when the alphabet will have run out of letters,
and the year that's halfway over
still has no direction. And the bank won't wait.

Accounts

The noose tightens. How much for each foot of rope,
each inch of neck, and the boxwood coffin,
who paid for lunch and was drink taken,
and how much to pay the hangman's wages?

Sir: my business was slow, my cash flow
sluggish, my credit withered long ago,
my only product in these words that light me
dimly through the dark not in much demand.

And I've no other skill. Words, figures: cold,
untouchable and abstract, logging receipts, payments,
goods in goods out, plus, minus. I might have been
bookkeeper in some distant trading station,

Reykjavik it will be called, forty years
shivering in the tight mouthed service
of the Northmen, entering and tallying,
and that because I was a boy who wrote.

Meanwhile to one side, late, through the long north light
I write the plot later called *Hamlet*:
a brother's poison and a wife's betrayal,
the son's dilemma as to vengeance, justice, silence,

and the last act always bloody carnage.
Then back to the profit and the loss
of journeys, dreams, chance encounters
with the other strangers, till all the words

that wondered at the world came down to this:
final demands from the Department of Wishful Thinking,
the bottom line, the exact amount now due
I cannot pay.

Brief encounter on the Yellowdog

Our man is sitting at a bar among reflections,
bits of himself he glimpses in the mirrors,
mopping the spilt drink of all his life,
rings on his fingers, keys at his hip, labels
in his lapels and maybe one day he'll be one
of the many tales he tells, he'll settle down
in far off Aberdeen and write a paperback,
he'll call it *Lost in Space* by Justin Thyme.

Outside: Aldgate in the rain. In here the music
is some song of a lost love, the barman says
ask me what you want, ask me if I'm working.
Dry Chablis she will have, he a half a bitter.
The trains are late, the signals on the blink.
They talk of distance, valleys of bells.
The deep sleep of wine and woodsmoke. Figs.
Apples. Vines climbing the Tuscan sunlight.

Nothing's happening as usual with everything.
Everyone as usual is somewhere else, these two
exploring each other and the Algarve,
the bartender back home on the Boyne,
the music somewhere on the road and our man
Curleytoes is rafting down the river
with the painted hostiles all around,
and that's the moment all their eyes meet.

It's called the here & now. He belts out
Oh the times we had below the snowline,
we lived the life of the river there,
women sharp and skinny as the reeds, our kids
spooning up the bony soup of winter.
Oh I was never sober, I was never drunk,
I stayed out of the army & out of the nick.
So don't collide with me I'm a solid object.

On the Yellowdog it's winter again, the music
in his brain wolf and coyote, a wheel spinning
round and around in its rut. *Oh Billy*
can your drool, can you sit up on a stool,
can you piss into the pot Little Billy?
This customer has eaten too many tomatoes.
He is no longer in touch with his despatcher.
What he has is a bad case of mad social worker.

Let's call it failed author syndrome. He has a dream.
He can see it all the time on the big screen
in his head. He'd settle for a dry goods store
somewhere at the edge of town, day by day
adding up the takings, home by 6 to the wife
and the Yellowdog River but it's time,
friend, time to go now, in the piddling rain.
Time to disappear to Planet Zero.

The bad news

And so it comes to this: didn't get the job,
didn't get the loan, didn't get the fifteen quid
my brother Novak owes me nine years now,
and don't qualify for the dole, so I quit.

Never a lucky ticket in the state lottery,
never me shouting *bingo bingo bingo*,
and once again I didn't win the pools,
and I'm getting old for this, too old.

Everyone here is dreaming of somewhere else.
Everyone here works at the heritage museum,
visited by people they can't somehow like
and their bossy knowledgeable children.

Not a lot to dream: age & Sir Death,
farewell to the stars, the swallows and the afternoon;
the young are swarming in over the beach stones,
dispossessed, impatient. And that's the good news.

So all the treaties are off and I'm mean as muddy water.
This is bad news day, this is a no deposit no return day,
and though I'm prudent as the Kings of Prussia
truth is I'm an act of desperation turning grey.

Film noir

Titles that are more properly stage directions. Then glimpses, snapshots, faces on streets, in doorways, in photographs and magazines, in films, in dreams, in shadow, in broad daylight: the occasions of their faces, what they say.

We're still sifting the evidence, bits of film, pages from books, manuals of instruction, catalogues, documents that have all been through the shredder. With their customary revolutionary zeal our students piece them together, patiently, haphazardly, matching letter with alphabet, line with line, a grand spaghetti of internal memoranda, minutes, shorthand notes, requisitions, letters, rosters, countersigned orders, demands, receipts, lists of stores. Ours is a strange archaeology, often inaccurate, barely articulate, the meanings of words forever shifting in translation, frame never matching frame, page page, so there is often no continuity, no sequence, no satisfyingly continuous narrative, indeed, sometimes no apparent meaning at all in these activities other than our persistence, without which nothing makes any sense at all.

Beginning again with a line heard in the street

Beginning anywhere at all with anything,
overheard on the underground: *Birth control?*
She never had any. A note taped to a window:
lost keys ask inside or *just get me a taxi,*
and the door smacked shut. Words found
on water I ferried home, subject to scribble
and sea bile. Yes I vaguely remember Amsterdam.

Today begins my letter to the Galicians,
dated this day on the Greenwich meridian,
Lord Alfred older now home from the grand tour,
confronting at last the blankness of the page,
an empty blue whose sky will surely fill,
a mouth wide open saying anything at all:
last seen by the river talking to a man.

Another day another dollar

Rails and their stations, nights, trains,
home again home again to this sweet black coffee,
here in my own small corner with my pussycat.
Let me tell you why I don't like this music.
Ah to be in England, the sweet impossibility
of communication, all this English babble
babble babble: *bad dog, keep off, no ball games.*

I recall the quiet Amish in their buggies,
carpenters who paint their front doors blue
for their marriageable daughters, living
along the borders of states. For them exile
is just across the river at Auntie Mattie's,
and everywhere the same elegant white birches,
through the mist the deer on delicate tall hooves.

Scenes from metropolitan life

I have been conversing with my old mate,
Andrew-by-the-Wardrobe, one day they say
he'll be a saint among the saints, mumbling
through the traffic and the office blocks
with all he owns in fifteen plastic bags,
and he the curator of abandoned churches,
his simple prayers the sounds stars make.

And yet with me all he ever talks is horses,
horses and beer. And women. How he loved
dancing with strangers, how he covets them still,
their sleek loveliness, knowing they won't last,
won't stay, roses in the rain, laughter
at the stair-end, leaving their shampoos
in the bathroom, and their pink aromas.

The lives of the saints

This one with the tight eyes, *Lorenzo*
he calls himself, *the Magnificent*,
chewing at the inside of his lip,
keeping his act up. All day on the bridge
in the alcove built for a saint he's there
with his singsong *change, cambio,*
wechsel, drogga, wearing Dante's face
and the comic's wall eye leading off
into the sky as he lifts your wallet,
and it's your own fault, tourist.

There is the long life of the window,
the interminable history of a doorway
that opens into poplared distance –
the Arno I had dreamed of, the old light,
some comfort in the furniture of time,
a little continuity perhaps. And there's
Lorenzo, sharp eyed and finger quick,
here where he's always been upon the bridge,
believing as he does in shorter odds
and a free market economy. Him I don't trust.

The maker of fakes

He opens his hands, shrugs. He says
What I make is all fake, there's no
song and dance. Let's say it's a Thursday.

We are walking down into the city
through the late night cars, drunks,
the cleaning squad in yellow dayglo.

Let's say the ambulance is wailing
its two notes *poor boy, poor boy,*
bleeding, dying. Let's say his name

is Leonardo, the maker of instruments,
all fake, a man I seldom meet, for both us
this is how it is here: grainy, fleeting.

He continues: *As to this instrument*
by which I am accused yes it is my making
though how became it a Capela, so sold
and listed, why that I cannot tell you.

Johannes from Dresden

A tall lamp. My face I bear high
through the strange world, a standard.
This face from the Thirty Years War
it is ordinary, a copy of thousands.

The only one I have to look out from.
Faces like mine framed in this yellow hair
died in thousands in the firestorm of 1945
sent by your Bomber Harris. They died

the deaths of the snails, of the ants,
the woodlice they shared the space with.
The flies. Thank you. I will not take a drink.
Not now. Not this time. Perhaps again.

Insomnia 1, 2, 3

Sometimes you can knock yourself out
taking whatever it takes to get wherever it is
and you do it, for hours, and for hours
you try out the trick called not being there
and maybe you sleep and maybe you drift
but you wake anyway on a dead chicken pillow
with a rat in your brain and a bat in your mouth
and though you clean each one of your teeth,
paste on a face that will just about do,
you still can't remember still can't recall
the numbers and names of each drop of the rain.

Something is missing, something is wrong:
that stain on your shirt, is it yours?,
that dark in your face, that trace of a voice
overheard at the moment you dived into silence
out of the clock-driven bird balmy universe
back of the Nostar Hotel of night plumbing and thumps –
that voice that said but what did it say, those words
those beautiful shards, they won't be back now.
Think. Drink hot black tea, black coffee.
Think of the sea. Think of the sweet shift of wheat
with the wind gone through it, just as the sea is.

The emigrant

A hundred miles from home, by the road
the crow's heavy alighting, the first buds
of spring yellowing towards the south.
My name is Stickincraw, my black looks
a mirror of the landscape, all around me
the same rain-stippled misery, northern uplands
I have prowled grinding out my excuses,
my fury at dumb rocks, sheep, bracken,
my short and stocky people, always a wild
mad strand of hair in the long east wind,
all my days it seems. Oh I worked,
mending wall, hedging and ditching
with my father's tools. But the worm
is in them now, and I am leaving.

Filmclip: Leningrad, October 1935

Dark comes early, and wet snow.
The citizens hurry from work,
scarfed, buttoned, thinking of supper,
the tram clanking and squealing
in whose glass an arm has wiped
a V of lit space wherein smoke,
old and young wrapped for winter,
eyes focussed somewhere ahead,
dreaming perhaps of a sausage,
of bread, coffee, a warm bed,
a bullet in the back of the brain.
Then they're gone. Next comes
the future. It looks like the past.

A survivor's memoir
(after Jerzy Kmiecik)

Another day on the slow trains south,
yellow sand to the sky's distant edge
then the River of Mystery brought us
to *Ak Metchet*, the White Palace, called
after the comrades came through Kazakhstan
Kizil Orda, the Red Capital, its names
at the station painted one over the other.

Here nothing to eat therefore nothing to steal.
And so to Tashkent that means Stone City,
Samarkand biscuit yellow, still in my dreaming.
I was by then again without shoes, a hole
the wind poked. That was 1942, the spring,
years from home, prison wire, prison trains,
a few necessary words the heart remembers.

By the Master of Jakabfalva, 1480
(for Miklos Zelei)

It is a wild place beyond the town wall:
the moment between moments when the blade
slits these two in their shifts into saints,
one already to his eternity of *Hallelujah*,
the other, Josias, James, brave before the blow.
Their faces say they thought as much.

Hooded, the two officials barely look,
each the shamefaced witness of the other,
come to see the job done, sign the paper,
make their report and turn into stones.
At the centre the executioner in black,
the ballet of his legs dancing to the blade.

No reply from the East

The mail addressed *Occupant* returns *Gone*,
all night the phone rings, no one answers,
at the stair's end again laughter, thuds,
then *Christ Almighty* they were saying

in those upraised fists of stone. By morning
they have renamed the streets, the wings
are missing from the statue of Victory,
the currency abandoned. And no bread.

So who were they to be in any case –
sour children forever in the blighted garden,
sweet innocents the others laughed at,
an embarrassment to their grandchildren?

I send you these letters I get no replies,
I tell you my secrets they're all of them lies.

His epistle to the Tatars
(for Ravil)

Friend from a distant country,
Asia and its horsemen. Elegant,
the white birches, through the white mist.

Last night I dreamed of Russia,
snow and a slow train to the mountains,
the taiga cluttered with plinths,
empty pillars, monuments to the empire
of electricity and state power and concrete.
In the high cold a man suddenly said
in plain English *but we're always alone.*

So now what, mon ami, now the planet's broken
and the People's Republic of Paradise kaput,
now the frontier is everywhere and everyone
on it a stranger? In my case I suspect
I have come to the end of my saying,
whatever that wildness was, and doubt
what I saw when I saw in such moments
lost itself in the photograph, faded out
among the vocabularies.

Inshallah.

God willing we'll be here when God willing
you return. And if not, when this face
I wear won't be my own may you think of me
sitting in a café, some place the lights
burn late till someone blows them out.

Poem ending in frogs

Meanwhile in the lands to the east, business
or no business or no business at all, no work
and the bread and jam factory closed down,
its redundant angels shaving their skulls
and it's Siegheil season again, old footage
with its soundtrack of broken bottles.

As usual it's raining on one side of the road,
there's forty years of ruin on the other,
and an ageing man is leaning into the wind
walking West with a dewdrop on his nose
halfway on the long road to Paris
from Novisibirsk, halfway through his life.

Here nothing and silence and listening to blackbirds,
the window blinds shuttering, wittering
in the hot wind of the time of the clowns
with Kalashnikovs, whispering *staatsicherheits
sicherheits staasi staasi*, still listening, adrift
in the pollen heavy air. Or they're hiding in the swamp
with the frogs, and round their necks bells
that don't ring, whistles that don't blow any more.

Here the Plough swings overhead and all night
in and out of the water of moon and mosquitos
the frogs make frog speech, soliloquy and chorus
of *You. Yes you. Oh you. You you you. You. You.*

You and you and you and you and you and you and you.

Essential Serbo-Croat

Guraj	Push
Pomozi mi	Help me
Boli	It hurts
Boli me	I have a pain
Boli me ovdje	I have a pain here
Bole me grudi	I have a pain in my breast
Bole me prsa	I have a pain in my chest
Boli me oko	I have a pain in my eye
Boli me stopalo	I have a pain in my foot
Boli me glava	I have a pain in my head
Hitno je	It's urgent
Ozbiljno je	It's serious
Boli me ovdje	It hurts here
Boli puno	It hurts a lot
To je jaka bol	It's a sharp pain
To je mrtva bol	It's a dull pain
To je uporna bol	It's a nagging pain
Vecinom vremena	Most of the time
Vrti mi se u glavi	I feel dizzy
Zlo mi je	I feel sick
Slabo mi je	I feel weak
Nije dobro	It's no good
Izgubio sam sve	I have lost everything
Ne mogu vam pomoci	I can't help you

Lovesong for Kate Adie

Wherever it's bad news is where she's from –
a bronze leathery sort of lady, dressed for disaster's season,
a tough mouth woman, and like me a nighthawk. Ah, Katie,

reporting from the barbed wire rims of hell,
Katie at the barricades I dream of nightly, her voice
a bell in the desert wind, her hair blown which way.

It's true she loves it out where the disputed air
is vicious with shrapnel, bullet stung, the night's
quick stink of sulphur, flies, dead camels, terror.

But I don't mind now if she never comes back to me,
so long as she's happy. The night in her is enough,
that long-ago voice sets my gonads galloping.

Sure I'm afraid for her and pray every evening at 6
for her flight to some quiet place, cool nights
and nightingales between earthquakes and insurrections.

There we meet again, the night bright with stars:
Plough, Pleiades, Pole Star. She drinks, laughs
her special laugh, turns to go. We fall into bed.

We fuck all night, Katie & me, I never flag,
she never wearies, we're drunk on whisky and each other
and sweet fresh rocky and who cares it's Thursday?

She's there for me. I'm here for her. Any day of the week.

The fat man's movie

I can see it now: a story about rich people,
a saga of three cars and two swimming pools,
the brother with too many wives, too many kids
who hate him already and all of them too much money.

Everyone else is a walkon, an easy sucker,
protagonists played by bad actors, a soap
that will run and run through prime time,
a blockbuster: plot, title: *The Fat Man's Tale.*

He starts out a poor refugee, an orphan
running before old grey footage of the war,
singing to himself *one ball, two small, none at all.*
He is a hero. He is given a medal. And so forth.

He goes bad, lives a swindler's life, a conman's,
a liar, a bully, a cheat, steals everyone blind.
At the end of his twisted rope he takes to the sea
in his private boat, calls up his private jet

for one last salute to his fat greedy vanity,
one last flypast, one last upright two fingers
to the universe and to you and to me. Remember
he's out there on the ocean and no one is looking,

no one to envy him, none to impress. And then
he slips off the boat and bobs off on the sea,
a fat drowned crook winched out of the water
and bundled offstage, swiftly buried in the holy city.

Probably in three parts. Coltrane for the lead,
to be played with deep integrity. Faye
to play the woman who tries to save him, the angel
weeping in the last reel, on the Mount of Olives.

Task 17

1 Remove webbing
2 Release smock waist velcro fasteners
3 Decontaminate gloves
4 Raise smock hem above trouser waistband
5 Untie braces
   Pull clear of loops
   Tie ends together
6 Release trouser waistband velcro fastener
7 Pull trousers down to knees
8 Decontaminate gloves again and remove them (inners included)
9 Store gloves in pocket
10 Adjust inner clothing
   Crouch and reach round behind to pull braces to one side
11 Defecate
12 Stand up
   Adjust inner clothing
   Decontaminate hands
13 Replace gloves
   Adjust nuclear biological chemical clothing

Practice
Read the study notes

Practise the procedures for urination and defecation wearing the full kit

Urination and defecation should only be attempted in areas set aside for the purpose

Women should follow the procedure for defecation for both bodily functions

Toilet paper must be protected from contamination

There are modified procedures for urination and defecation in the Arctic. If you are equipped to operate in the Arctic check with your NBC instructor for details of the modified drill

Task 18: The unmasking procedure

What you have to know and do

You have to:

- Know the general procedure for unmasking

- Carry out the sniff test

Tasks 17 and 18 from the British Army Nuclear Biological Chemical Warfare Training Manual *Survive to Fight* (D/DAT/13/33/18, Army Code 7133)

Positive Identification

Their eyes they were grey blue they were black nothing.
One had a scar a burn a birthmark one an earring one a tattoo
dotted across through over his neck and the legend *cut here*.
That makes two were there two was it 3? One with the headbutt
one with the fists and the finger rings one with a fancy blade.
One a white male one a girl one something quick I didn't see.
One a bully one a sissy and one who was an absolute bastard.
One with a knife one a razor one with a baseball bat.
One that wept the other one screaming and screaming
at the same time someone someone else laughing out loud.
I found pain pain however when wherever it comes hurts.
They all yelled the same kind of words you know them
the same mad anger the same eyes the same dead smile
the same fury at someone long ago dead yesterday perhaps.
One was white one black one some other shade of human.
I recall as I fell for the umpteenth last maybe time
my thought here in this great multi-ethnic society
you can be beaten and robbed you can die by all sorts
for all sorts of reasons for none by all sorts of exotics.

The Chicken Variations

Chicken calling:

Whisky Oscar Chicken. Whisky Oscar Chicken
calling Foxtrot, come in Foxtrot.

This is Whisky Oscar Chicken
calling Foxtrot, come in Foxtrot.

Chicken faith:

The word was let there be chicken.
Before the chicken was the chicken,
before the egg was the egg,
from the beginning of the word the word was chicken.

And before that the word was egg.
And before that the word was still egg.
And before that the great sky chicken
who is the rooster and hen mother of us all.

Phrases for translation:

Excuse me, parlez-vous chicken ici?
Please, where is the cambio for live chickens?
Is this the fast chicken for Bratislava?
Bitte, do you have a place I can leave my broody hen?
I am married with a roost and three chicks,
I live in Little Red Rooster Town, Minnesota.
I was born in the Year of the Chicken
under the sign of the Chicken, have a nice day.
I would like chicken en suite, por favor.
Chicken on the rocks, chicken all round.
It's my turn for the Lakenvelder meine Damen und Herren.
S'il vous plaît m'sieur I want the Chicken Cab Co.
I would like a bottle of this Chateau Poulet Blanc.
This chicken is too loud, take it away please.
Entschuldige, I have to go buy a chicken now.
Pardon me, I think my chicken is on fire.
I have a one way ticket to Chickenville, goodbye.

Let us consider the chicken:

Lately I've been thinking about the chickens,
clucking their peevish lives out in the long batteries,
where the lights shorten the days, nothing changes,
it's hell on earth and every one in here is loo-loo.

Even in a yard they fret, always at the edge,
suspicious, laying the great egg, staring, watching,
wary for the cockbird or pecking at their dinners
or asleep dreaming worms, slugs, fat maggots.

And then they die, all of them without names,
numbers, without biographies, votes, pension rights,
their throats routinely cut, stripped, chopped up,
cooked in a pot with onions and peppers and devoured.

Chuck. Chuck. The Hungarians, who got them
from the Bulgarians, they say *tyuk. Tyuk tyuk tyuk.*
Comrades, clearly this is not in the chickens' interest.
Our feathered friends are manifestly at a disadvantage.

And no one protests, no one gives a gypsy's gob
for all their aspirations, dreams, their brief itchy lives
scratching and complaining, part of the food chain.

Save the chicken. Save the chicken.

Chicken lore:

For a start there was the Miracle of the Cocks and Hens,
there was the Parable of the White Leghorn,
there was the Cockadoodledoo Revelation at Alexandria,
there was the Exemplary Lesson of the Rhode Island Reds,
there was the Sermon on the Flightless Gallinacae,
there was the Bantam Capon Culture of the Po Valley,
there was the Black Langshan Khanate of Kiev,
there was the Coxcomb Dynasty of the Mekong Delta,
there was the Teaching of Salvatore Stefano Cacciatore,
there was the Red Rooster Crusade of 1332,
there was the Most Noble Order of Jersey Black Giants,
there was the Barred Plymouth Rock Declaration,
there was the Constitution of the Andalusian Blues,

47

there was the Divine Sisterhood of Old Poultry Lane,
there was the secret conclave of the Orpington Buffs,
there was La Fleche, Crevecoeur, Campine, Faverolle,
there was the whole mighty host of Gallus Domesticus
migrating out of the east, crossing the windy steppes
clutched in the armpits of savage horsemen,
and there was blood, there were mountains of skulls.
We were at Marathon, at Agincourt, on the Somme,
we were the Wild Chickens who fought at Malplaquet.
We too had our epics, our ten year return to Ithaca
only to find strangers clucking in our compound.
We too had our blind poets Homer and Milton.
There was Chaucer's *The Dream of Fair Chickens*,
there was the last lay of the Fighting Cocks,
there was the Black Virgin of the Chickenshack,
there was Shakespeare's famous Chicken Soliloquy,
there was the patriarch Chicken Joe Bailey,
there was the saint and martyr Adolphus Chicken,
there was the inventor and explorer Gustavus Chicken,
there was the hero Lieutenant General Gordon Chicken,
there was Captain Bingo 'Chickenwings' Benson
who saved us again and again from foreign invasion,
there was the gunfighter Roaring Jack Chicken,
there was the horn player Willy Bantam Chicken,
there was the Ode to a Chicken and the Air on a Chicken,
there was the Chicken Sonata, the Chicken Symphony,
there was Chicken Blues, there was Chicken Boogie,
there was the Chicken Domesday, the Cockcrow Manifesto
the Chicken Coop Oath, the Last Address to the Chickens,
there was the chicken round dance and chicken chants,
there were chicken fiestas and chicken olympics,
there was Chicken Rococo and Chicken Gothic,
there was the Colegio Pollo of medieval Florence,
there were the *Chicken Études* of Guillaume Apollinaire,
there was the School of Contemporary Chicken Studies,
there was the Distressed Indigent Chickens' Benevolent Society,
there were the Thoughts of The Cocksman Chairman Charlie,
there was the Theory and Evolution of the Chicken,
there was the architecture of Frank Lloyd Chicken,
there was Henry Ford's Chicken Mass Production System,
and it says here much else besides, all of it now best forgot.

Saith the Sky Chicken:

Woe to those who sell guns
amongst the warring states.
Woe to those who shell the wounded.

Woe to those who take another's house,
and say *this is my farm, these my chickens,*
who pick up the photo album and say
why these are all my relatives.

Interim conclusions:

What is a mere chicken to do?
Everything you see belongs to the Fat Man.
The true commonwealth of equals is now very far off.
The Dark Ages begin again any time now.

I'll tell you this: the Hundred Years War
did nothing for those who eat worms.
What use was the Renaissance?
The Revolution's been and gone.

Last bulletin:

The barbarians are at the city's throat,
their tanks moving down the great ringroads,
the anti-chicken forces are all around us.
Any second now there will be no more electricity.

This is the end of the Chicken Road.
This is the last hour of the Chicken Republic.
This is the final demise of the Chicken Revolution.
This is the end of all chicken civilisation.

And this is Radio Free Chicken signing off.
Goodbye Foxtrot, Goodbye Tango Charlie.
We of the Chicken Coalition salute you.
We of the Chicken Millennium bid you adieu.

Her mirror

Sideways it always was along the long wall
and I still see her in it though she's gone now,
combing her hair, setting her face right for the street.

I fixed it upright by my door to watch who comes,
who passes. Things are not so easy in this neck of the woods.
The neighbourhood's gone crazy.

But in Milly's mirror all the world's reversed –
car numbers, faces, turned around as mirrors do,
and the mad didikais raging in the street all night.

They beat each other up, they're selling crack.
They brick each others' cars and windows
and they scream all night through the night furnace.

Milly's mirror watches.
Milly's mirror watches all.

The road to Henrietta's house

Well there's a lot of ways to get there a lot of ways to go.
For a start you can stop off at the Rainbow Café and drink
drink yourself beyond yourself into silence through the jukebox
through all the chatter of the pinball machines till its *Time*.

That would be the end of it that would be the tale. But suppose.
Suppose you have the one drink leave set out across the city.
You take the bus you take the tram you take the train you walk.
You come to the river there you wake the sleepy boatman.

For sure for certain he's sure in a foul mood, and sore drunk.
And when he's rowed you over there's the marshes and the wild
       beasts.
There's the vipers and the soldier ants and the roaches and the flies.
You have to catch your own wild horse you have to tame it, ride it

at last at long last down the long road to Henrietta's house,
and just because all hell has broken broken loose broken loose
you're thinking someone something in the universe doesn't want
the two of you to meet, ever. Suppose you just keep going

to the end the road makes in the door that opens into light
water in the kettle wine in the dark red bottle and her beads.
And now she wants to dance she wants to click her fingers laugh
fling out her braids flying in the window in the candle's flame.

In praise of vodka

The taste they say for they must
or they feel that they must so they say
so they say they say *it has none*,
there's no taste, just water.

Water: the glassy lake Christ trod,
a bowl Herod rinsed his fingers in,
the rain falling on Troy's ruins,
last word last balm of the living.

The same water, over and over. They say
for they say for they must so they say
we're running out running dry but there's always
the same amount as there's always been.

It's we who are more. As for myself
I've spent all my days working out
just what little Miss Peaches might like
and I'm due a day off for the rest of my life.

So out of the freezer the bottle, the green
frosty bottle, its label iced in cyrillic,
the glass and the water beside the glass.
Russische. Moskovskaya. Stolichnaya.

So this is the taste of nothing:
nothing then nothing again. Nothing at all.
The taste of the air, of wind on the fields,
the wind through the long wet forest.

A stream and the rain. I lie in my yard
and open my mouth to the moon and the down falling rain
and the rods of its words speak over my tongue
to the back of my throat and they say

Voda
Water
Vodka

Voda
Water
Vodka

Voda
Water
Vodka

Voda
Water
Vodka

Voda
Water
Vodka

The carpenter's confession

All these years something grew in me, measuring,
cutting good wood, stitching my own sweet way with a dowel,
a nail, a joint, reassembling the forest into chairs
and cupboards in a room swollen with wood dust.

This was the page of my life. Then I was redundant.
So I come out to Wanstead most days, to the Flatts,
brooding briar and star moss, lichen, the ways of the ants
and the birds, if the day holds the rain off.

Most days in the city's diet of sound I'm deaf in one ear,
in the other intermittently lucid on the left hand channel,
clairvoyant and amplified, the system working at last,
both speakers straight to the brain's right side.

So today.

Today I lay watching a red kite rise and fall
in the shimmer of the updraughts, hearing
the far away laugh of the boy at the string's end:
to him everything an amazement, like new made money.

And the wind through all easy. I pondered the weather,
and what waterlogged secrets the gravel ponds keep,
what guns and what corpses and why, when the day's good
and nothing should wreck it some fool always does.

So today, I brought my Kalashnikov.

Away to one side sunlight was moving on towers
in Leyton and Leytonstone. Gulls, crows, one then
two magpies in the scribble of weeds. And the city
tuned itself out, its traffic a distant barking and child sounds.

As usual as ever I was taking a last backward glance
at the world's green spatter of leaves, wind
haunting the grass, high up and invisible the larks'
rusty twittering, overhead an incoming plane in descent

where the captain had just flipped the no smoking sign.
Traffic noise began rolling in, sirens, then the buzz
of some model plane's toy motor round and around
in the slow light that but for him would be bliss.

So today I put in a clip. Today I took off the safety.

The man who ran away from the circus

That one with the haircut round his ears,
the one that grins with the teeth and the glasses,
the little man holding a long umbrella –
or whichever one he is he's the shorter of the two.

It's been a hard road he says. As a kid
he remembers they were always on the move.
He'd sneak away to do his homework in the Fat Lady's tent.
He remembers ropes, sawdust, llama spit, camel stink.

And he remembers how it was with his dad
on a bad night of muddy rain and a hatful of unsold tickets,
the takings slithering off into expenses, the books
unbalanced on the table and the whisky bottle out,
the dogs howling in the yard. Lenny the lion's sick
and the liontamer out on the razzle with the man/woman.
The ringmaster's run off with the cashflow
and the clowns are demanding a payrise and a pension
and Christmas is coming, it's all they can do
to find hay for the horses.

He's at the end of his endless tether again.

About then the old man would straighten up, pour a drink,
fix his bow-tie and collar, clear his throat,
look you right in the eye and say *There are signs
things are getting better. We're beginning to see
an upturn in our fortunes at last. The confidence rate
is well up this month. There are indications the worst
of this long bitter recession is over.*

That's how it was then. It was either that
or close down the zoo, sell the elephant,
auction off the tigers and the freak sheep,
the sideshows and the performing monkeys,
turn the zebras into handbags, the horses into glue,
lease the big top and develop the site, retire to Brighton
to sell takeaways, become a deck chair attendant,
watch the cricket and the bowls and the grey swilltub sea
from a window in his favourite seafront pub
and reminisce: *ah the good old days of the classless society,*
the world of every opportunity where everyone
could get to crack the whip. That again.

And he's away. Again the horses prance into the ring,
the pompons and the big drum and the trombone's oompah oompah
and the girls glittering in fishnet and sequins.
Here come the stiltmen and the clowns, the jugglers
and the human cannon ball, the rubber man, the singing dog,
the giant and the dwarf and the thinnest man in England,
JoJo with her instruments and Suzy's little tricks,
the man who throws axes, the man who swallows knives
and the one who breathes fire, Manolito's highwire act
from Andalusia, the Russian pyramid, the invisible American,
the drunks, the grand finale of the troupe of South American
        pickpockets
that did him in at last. Them and all those women.

Interrogating the egg-timer

Born?

I was born in a paper bag in the basement of a shark,
in a windstorm in Arizona, in a Turkish shebeen,
in the cold blue corner of an isosceles triangle.
I was a child of the union of rain and whisky.

How much of my beginning can I remember?

Why, isn't this it? I remember nothing and everything.
There was a blue sky. For once my father was happy.
My mother was a test tube but more fruity.
I find the world fairly round, roundly and profoundly unfair.

You ask about my last life, the one before this.

As I recall I travelled in the suitcase
of a man always stopping to call long distance.
I was the ashtray of a perverted monk,
I was alone I was always alone.

You want to know how long this road I'm on is?

Listen, 60 minutes is the end of my attention-span.
Anything beyond and it's head-over-heels
I'm in love again with someone's juices and aromas.
You've read Lawrence. You'll know what I mean.

My favourite food is anything.

If I stopped eating altogether I'd be a very slim hourglass.
I'm so tired of salt with everything.
I'll just go on being turned over and over,
living out my life in quiet three minute orgasms.

Where did I spend last night? Pass.

Am I capable of transformation? Well,
I can turn energy into raw mountains of detritus.
I am capable of anything. Everything again.
Again nothing. I want to go back into my box now.

Ailments? I catch cold when I need to.

No tobacco, no alcohol, no drugs. Up at dawn,
jogging on the spot, somersaults. I keep myself neat,
ready for action. *Intrepid* is my middle name.
In my job down at the harbour I guide the boats in.

You want to know how I work?

First I have to be turned over. Then
I walk up and down staring at nothing,
thinking of nothing in particular.
Serendipity. A certain aimlessness. Theft.

Betimes I am madde as anie hattere.

Certainly I get sick of the company of Young Smartarse
and his mates, I am a morose and solitary drunk.
I take this ambience from a man called Waits.
I take it and I give it back again.

No, I never watch old movies. I am one.

At what time do I burst into blossom?
Whenever I dance, when I grow up.
Actually I'm in bloom now. Can't you see?
All these pink buds will be shiny green apples one day.

My favourite position is 90 degrees upright.

How did it feel to be taken away by thieves?
Terrific, I love travel. I adored them,
they were all excellent dancers, good talkers.
They taught me advanced kleptomania and secrecy.

When did I masturbate? I could ask you the same thing.

I'm old enough not to be daft enough to answer that.
You want to know what happened to my seven sisters?
That would be Melissa and the others, Sugar Plum,
Stanley Knife, Consonant, Tin Can, Marzipan

and the other one that was never called anything.

They're the Sisters Pleiades now. Can't you see them
all around me? They were all abused by Father Time.
As to my future life I just plan to keep busy.
Busy and useful till the salt runs out.

Then I expect to be a hand or just a finger.

When I speak to the police what will I tell them?
All these questions. I'll say I'm no stool pigeon.
I'll tell them how unbearable you've been,
they should lock you up for life. I'll spit salt at them.

So how would you feel after a thousand nights without sleep?

What does freedom mean to me? My favourite tipple,
the same as my religion: everything I see.
Taking longer to change. When there's
nothing else in the world I can rape.

And what do I mean by 'I'm in love again'?

Well, I was bored in the supermarket.
The top half of my glassy body loves my bottom half.
It's my normal status. In any case
I was dried out, I'd drunk six cups of coffee.

I don't know I'm no intellectual.

I was in love before. She gave me a ring.
That ended in a jackdaw's nest. She gave me white crystal.
I gave her only my time. And what now?
Well, I could write a cheerful book about graveyards.

I could start a small war.

I could drive the peasants out of Thuringia,
lob mortars onto hungry people in a Sarajevo bread queue.
I'd rather dance though. I'd rather the company of books,
candlelight, unaccompanied singing. Fact is

I'm an officer and gentleman in the SAS. I kill people.

I can mumble the Lord's Prayer in Anglo-Saxon.
And the riddles: what am I now, pray? Answer:
a long falling through myself into a pile of whiteness,
the cone of ashes of the dead at Birkenau.

What do I expect of strangers?

That they keep close to the walls. Water, bread, a small fish.
Just slipping in and out of time. I'm content
passing the salt from one half to the other of myself.
This time the answer is *Edelweiss-Piraten gegen Nazis.*

And who would I run to? Who indeed.

The mad. The imprisoned. The condemned. The dead.
Anyone who starts the day without a good breakfast.
There are four of us in here you know,
one for each season. And more to come.

What are my dreams? Wanderers. Other dreamers.

By the end of the week I'm more a smell than a flavour.
There are those to whom I bear the debt of time,
guttural people. I myself am clear glass,
falling white crystals. Drop me and I break and that's *Amen.*

What am I weary of? I'll tell you.

Eggs, for one thing. Quotations from Shakespeare.
The Books of Exodus and Leviticus. Answering questions.
Flying the Atlantic. All of Disney.
The words *arabesque, fraught,* and *binocular.*

I'm weary of a life without legs.

Unaccompanied singing

À capella: unaccompanied singing, as in a chapel, from Latin *cap-ella*, a diminutive of *cappa*, cape, referring to the chapel built to house the relic of the cape of St Martin of Tours (316-397?), Patron Saint of France. Born in the Roman province of Pannonia, now in Western Hungary, he was forced into the army at 15 where he became a Christian and an early conscientious objector. Thrown into prison, he was discharged at 20, and shortly thereafter came the incident for which he was to be revered, when, at Amiens, he split his cloak with a beggar. Later he became a hermit at Poitiers, and was unwillingly chosen to be bishop of Tours, to whom miracles were ascribed. It seems everything he did he did reluctantly, but for the matter of the cape. After his death the cape was adopted as the symbol of the Merovingian and Carolingian kings, and carried by them into battle. At the accession of the first of the Carolingians, the illiterate Peppin the Short, the task of drawing up royal documents was assigned to the *capellani*, chaplains of the *capella*, whose original duty had been to look after the cape and the chapel that housed it. And so from the name of a covering against the rain to the name for its sanctuary and its guardians, *capella* comes to stand for all chapels, for their servants, then for the singing that took place in them without music, the music only of human voices.

Sharing the same name is Capella, in the constellation Auriga, a binary star at 50 light years distance, the sixth brightest in the night sky, its name deriving, like the constellation Capricorn, aka the horned goat, tenth sign of the Zodiac – from Latin *capra*, nanny goat, in Greek myth a she-goat (or nymph) that nursed the infant Zeus.

So now we have a story of a star, a nanny goat suckling an infant god, a saint, a cape, a chapel, clerks, and singing.

Let's take the goat track.

Considering the various derivatives of the projected Indo-European root, *kapro-*, goat, leads on to Latin *caper*, goat, *capra*, she-goat; *caprifig*, the goat fig; *capric acid*, so named for its odour, presumably goatlike; *capella gallinago*, the common snipe; *capelin*, a species of smelt; *caber*, pole, from Gaelic *cabar*, from Vulgar Latin *caprio*, rafter, though the shift from goats to rafters as yet escapes me; *cabrilla* a tropical sea bass, presumably goat-looking, Spanish dim. of *cabra*; *cabriolet*, a two wheeled one horse carriage, from a French diminutive of *cabriole* from Latin *capreolus*, wild goat, referring presumably to the carriage's motion; *capriole*, an upward leap, all four hooves off the ground, made by a trained horse, through French from Italian *capriola*, leap of the goat; *capriccio* (Italian: *capo* + *ricchio* (hedgehog), literally 'head with hair standing on end' hence horror, or caprice); *chevron*, badge of rank, in heraldry an inverted V, in architecture a V shaped pattern, in Middle English from Old French a beam, a rafter, and so back to the caber and the capering goat once more, though I don't (yet) see how. But then *capreolate*, tendril like, again from Latin *capreolus*, wild goat, referring to the wooden prop supporting tendrils or vines – and (here it comes) the V shape cut at the top of the prop suggesting horns, a goat's horns, hence rafters, turned downward to support a roof, just as the letter A is the inverted diagram of the head of an ox. And might a cape be made of goatskin?

All this is speculative, the outcome of night-grubbing in the dictionaries. It reappears here and there as motif, hints at recurrent themes, lone voices, a chorus of unaccompanied singing that becomes an opera of fish, birds, leaping goats, vines and rafters, striped sergeants of infantry, kilted cabermen, horses and their trainers, the rattle of many tongues in capricious symphony. As for the parts the performers of this work will play, more night sifting throws up the Portuguese instrument maker, Antonio Capela, born 1932, a leading European maker of violins, violas and cellos. It reveals Sir Arthur Capel, beheaded in 1649, Royalist leader in the English Civil War, 'a man in whom the malice of his enemies could discover very few faults', whose escape from the Tower of London was betrayed by a boatman for 20 pounds. And so now we have a Judas. There's Andreas Capellanus, a twelfth-century French writer on courtly love, there's Martianus Minneus Felix Capella, an early fifth-century advocate at Carthage and writer on the rules of prose and poetry, there's a seventeenth-century Huguenot theologian and Hebrew scholar, Louis Cappel. There's a sixteenth-century Venetian noblewoman, Bianca Capello, beautiful, passionate, intelligent, the focus of intrigue and scandal, mistress and later wife of Francisco I de Medici, by the ruse of a fake pregnancy and a borrowed baby to deceive her lover into marriage. So much for romance. Soon after the marriage both died suddenly in their beds, of poison believed to have been administered by the Duke's brother. There's Luigi Capello, Italian general of World War I, and Giacomo Capellin, born 1887, a Venetian glassmaker who revived the glass industry at Murano, there's Heinrich Kapell, a seventeenth-century gunmaker of Copenhagen, and there's Johann Capeller, of Munich, around 1811 first flute in the King of Bavaria's court orchestra. And for the scenery, tempering the wild Italian with an ochre northern sobriety, there's Jan van de Cappelle, 1624-1679, Dutch painter of calm seascapes and silvery winter landscapes.

And so we begin with voices in the starry night singing without accompaniment. Then a flute, then a quartet of instruments fashioned by the Portuguese master, a chorus, characters, a plot that begins under a bright star with a suckling goat and the splitting of the saint's cape, rain and lightning and horses, scenes amongst the glassblowers and the gunmakers and the horse trainers, to one side the storming of advocates and grammarians and theologians, and all proceeding to betrayal for mere cash, despite the passionate temper of Bianca, the comedy of the baby trick, the mad speeches of the Italian general, resplendent in his plumes and braids, amidst the sombre Dutchman's winter roads and water, ships always in the offing.